WHO TAUGHT FROGS TO HOP?

A Child's Book about God

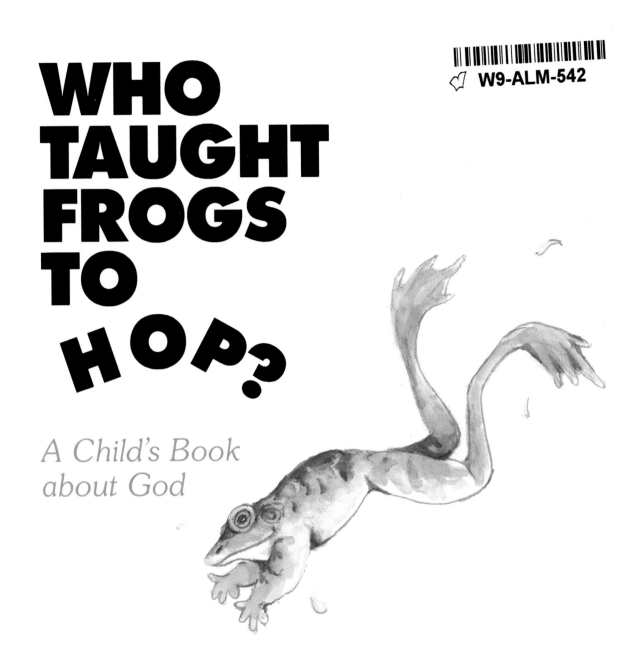

By Robert D. Ingram
Illustrated by June Goldsborough

AUGSBURG ● MINNEAPOLIS

For Chris, Matt, Deb,
and all the kids at Grace Church

WHO TAUGHT FROGS TO HOP?
A Child's Book about God

Copyright © 1990 Augsburg Fortress

LCCN 89-82552   ISBN 0-8066-2457-4

Manufactured in the U.S.A.   AF 9-2457

94   6   7   8   9   10

A NOTE TO PARENTS AND FRIENDS OF CHILDREN

Children delight in the world God has created. A frog splashing into a pond rivets their attention to the wonder of these green amphibians. And what child can resist a puddle, new shoes and all? *Who Taught Frogs to Hop?* allows children to associate all these delights with their source—our loving God.

As their imaginations play with creation, children can also play with you, the reader. As you assume the child's role of asking one question after another, they get to take the adult's role of providing the correct answers. The fact that every question you ask has the same answer—"God"—just reinforces the child's fun and emphasizes what is obvious to everyone, except for silly old adults!

This book is a playful way to teach a child about God and the good that God has created. You add the fun by reading playfully. And don't forget to add the kisses, tickles, and hugs at the right places too!

Whose idea was it to make the world round instead of square?

I like it round because it doesn't have any sharp corners. But who thought of it?

Do *you* know?

And who decided to use so many
different colors for flowers, rainbows,

birds,

fish,

butterflies,

beetles . . .

and all those funny-colored
bugs that want to sit
on my dish?

Who taught frogs
to hop
and land
with a
SPLASH?

Or monkeys
    to swing from limb to limb
        and tree to tree?

Or mountain goats
to never look down
when they
jump
from one high,
teetering rock
        to the next?

Who taught raccoons
to wash their
food?
Who taught squirrels
to store nuts for
winter?

And who taught
kangaroos to
raise babies
in their
pockets?

Who thought
up all this
neat stuff?

DO YOU KNOW?

Like, who thought of putting the crunch in apples?

The corn on the cob?

And the water in the melon?

Who thought up puddles
and ducks
　　and little kids splashing
in bare feet?

And who had the great idea of decorating
the night sky with all those twinkling stars?

Who taught cows
to say,

Mooooooo

Mooo

Mooo?

and owls to
say,
Who o o o o o ?
DO YOU
KNOW WHO O o o o o ?

Who thought up soft laps
and gentle arms
to hug you while you
listen to bedtime stories?

And whose idea
was it

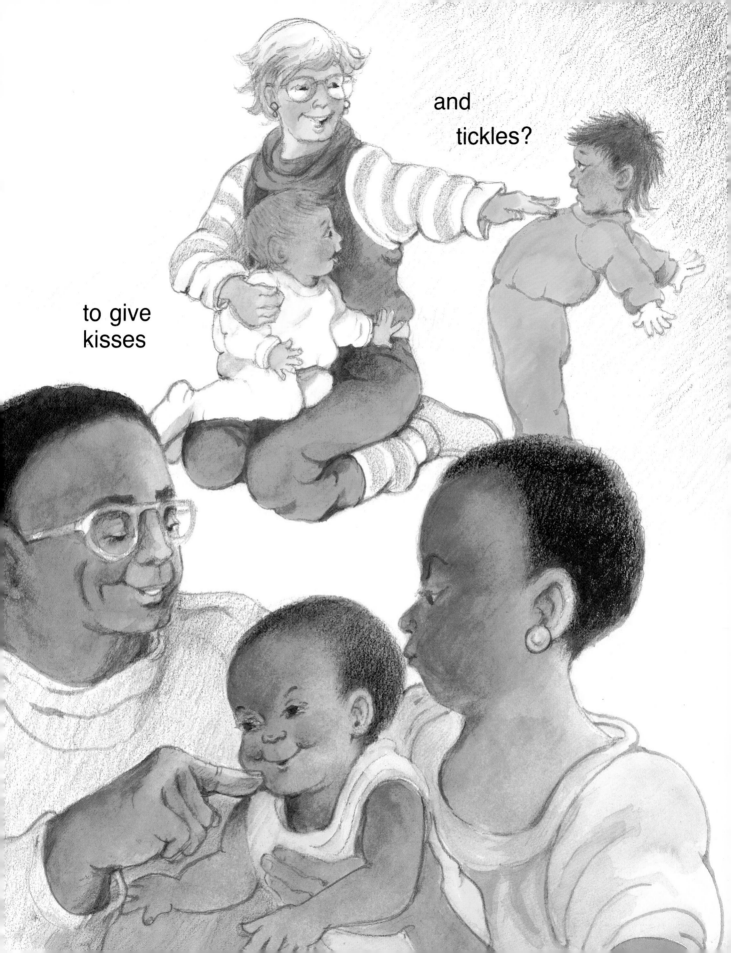

and
tickles?

to give
kisses

Who thought up
moms and dads,
       grandmas
              and
                     grandpas,
       aunts
              and
                     uncles,
       nieces, nephews,
cousins,
       and all
              the
                     rest?

Best
of
all,
who thought of

YOU?

May I say I think that
was a really,
really good idea?

Who came up with all these
wonderful ideas?
Do you know who?

If you do, then
do you know anyone better to sing
songs to in church?
    Or to say thank you to at the dinner table?

Or to love
for ever and

EVER AND EVER AND EVER AND EVER AND EVER AND EVER AND EVER AND EVER AND EVER AND EVER AND EVER AN

EVER AND EVER AND EVER AND EVER AND EVER AND EVER AND EVER AND EVER AND EVER AND EVER AND EVER AND EVER AND

EVER
AND EVER AND EVER
AND EVER AND EVER
AND EVER AND EVER
AND EVER AND EVER
AND EVER AND EVER

AND

EVER

AND

EVER

and EVER?!

My questions are done, but I
have something for you—
a great big hug
from me and
YOU
KNOW
WHO!